HIS HAMMOCK IN THE SHADE

by Connie Barngrover
(Coni)

Copyright © 2004 by Connie Barngrover

His Hammock In The Shade
by Connie Barngrover

Printed in the United States of America

ISBN 1-594674-05-1

All rights reserved by the author. The contents and views expressed in this book are solely those of the author and are not necessarily those of Xulon Press, Inc. The author guarantees this book is original and does not infringe upon any laws or rights, and that this book is not libelous, plagiarized or in any other way illegal. If any portion of this book is fictitious, the author guarantees it does not represent any real event or person in a way that could be deemed libelous. No part of this book may be reproduced in any form without the permission of the author.

Unless otherwise indicated, Bible quotations are taken from the New King James Version.

Book layout and graphics by: Naomi Krstinic
Editing and proofreading by: Mellanie Tuttle

DEDICATED TO

THOSE DESIRING TO TOUCH

THE FACE OF GOD

SPECIAL THANKS TO

my mom, Eileen Prier, for her faithful prayers that often kept her on her face long into the night, my friend Naomi who worked tirelessly with me to bring this to a finish, all of my family and friends who have encouraged me to write this book, and especially to my husband, Lyle, for his love and support for over 33 years. I love you, honey.

In loving memory to my father, Ray Prier, wish you were here to see it finished, dad.

CONTENTS PAGE

ABOVE THE STORM	1
ANOINTED ARCHER	3
ANSWER SEEDS	5
AWAITING YOUR CALL	7
BIRTH OF A NEW DAY	9
BLESSED BANKS	11
CHRISTMAS GIFTS	13
CIRCUMCISED HEART	15
CREATED TO FLY	17
CREATION SPEAKS OF LOVE	19
CRYING HEARTS HEARD	21
DO YOU HEAR HIM COMING?	23
EASTER MORN	25
FAITH'S VOICE	27
FATHER'S DELIGHT	29
FIRST THINGS FIRST	31
GIFTS TO GIVE	33
GO YE	35
GOOD MORNING LORD	37
HARD PLACES	39
HE IS	41
HIS HEALING HEM	43
HIS MAJESTY'S THRONE	45
HOLY SEED	47
IS YOUR MIDDLE NAME JONAH?	49
JESUS PRAYS FOR ME	51
JOURNEY TO HEALING	53
JUST WANTED YOU TO KNOW	55
LORD OF BLESSING	57
LOVING LIBERATOR	59
MERCY'S MISSION	61
MEETING PLACE	63
MY ALL IN ALL	65
NIGHT BATTLES	67
POTTER'S CLAY	69

CONTENTS (cont.)

PRECIOUS PEACE	71
SLEEPLESS KEEPER	73
SOMETIMES TEARS CAN SMILE	75
SPRING'S ESCORTS	77
STILLER OF THE STORM	79
TRUST IN TURMOIL	81
UNWAVERING WISDOM	83
VOICE OF SILENCE	85
WARRIOR ON THE HILL	87
WATCHFULL WARRIOR	89
WHISPER OF HIS SPIRIT	91
THE WORD IS GOD	93
NO MISTAKE	95
MY CHILD	98
AUTHOR'S NOTE	101
GOD'S LOVE PLAN	102
SALVATION VERSES	103

INTRODUCTION

Take a walk with me down the lane and around the bend. There it is. Do you see? It's just over there, past the gardenia bushes and off to the right. Oh, what a place.

Not many people know it is there. They are too busy trying to grab the brass ring, or working to hang another certificate on their already crowded wall.

Maybe they are just struggling to keep food on the table or stay one step ahead of the bill collectors. It could be that the noise of their loneliness pulls them into the cave of self-pity.

Who knows why only the few have found this sacred place, this place that is carpeted with the precious faces of wild flowers. This place is teeming with the handiworks of your loving Creator. One can see the busyness of the ladybugs as they dance on the multicolored petals.

You can't help but be comforted by the hum of the bees and the whisperings of the hummingbird's wings. Can you smell the sweetness of the honeysuckle? Can you feel the tiny breeze on your cheek as the butterfly twirls by?

Listen to the chorus of the wrens and the meadowlarks as they spread their wings in the sun to dry the morning dew. Oh, how holy it all is.

Your senses are alive, maybe for the first time in years. As you scan the tapestry before you, sensing there is yet an even holier place, your eye settles on that one tree set off in the distance.

    You find your feet quietly pressing forward as if being pulled by an invisible thread. Each step draws you deeper into a place that has been prepared just for you by the Father. Now you can see it, your destination. This is the place that has been calling to you from the time of your new birth, the place where your Comforter awaits. It's there before you, beckoning, wooing, and tenderly tugging you into itself.

    "HIS HAMMOCK IN THE SHADE" hangs from the largest branch of a majestic magnolia tree that has planted its roots deep into the banks of a singing brook. There is something wonderfully strange about this glistening white hammock, it looks to be a perfect fit for your weary body. Gently you ease yourself down and it wraps itself around you like a blanket, cradling you in His presence. Amazingly, a gentle breeze begins to stir, rocking you into a peaceful rest. As you release a sigh of contentment, you can hear that still small voice hover over you saying, "I am glad you are here, child. I have much to share, and you will not leave as you came."

    What great love the Father has for you to prepare this resting place, a place of solitude and safety, a place of watering and restoration, a place where all the noise is hushed.
Won't you let the gentleness of our Lord and Savior, Jesus Christ escort you from your place of unrest into His peaceful presence. Come and enter in, and touch the face of your God, for if you do you will never want to leave the soothing sway of
"HIS HAMMOCK IN THE SHADE."

"COME UNTO ME

ALL YOU WHO LABOR

AND ARE HEAVY LADEN

AND I WILL GIVE YOU

REST."

Matthew 11:28

ABOVE THE STORM

Knock and it shall be opened, seek and you will find,
All the power you need, to give you peace of mind

Keep your eyes on Me when trouble comes along
For only in My grace do you find your victory song

Do not look about you at the torment of the sea.
Hold fast to My garment and I'll pull you unto Me

Set your face like flint, refuse to cower in fear
For in My glorious presence My comforting voice you'll hear

No need to worry your heart and be consumed in dread,
For I'm your victorious King, in battle I'll cover your head

Keep your eyes from weeping and your soul from drawing back,
Trust in the hand of your God, Who gives you all you lack

There's not a mountain too big nor trial that's too grand
That cannot be reduced to a pebble in My hand

Let praise come from your depths in the darkness of your day
Trust in the God of glory Who faithfully lights the way

I've yet to lose a loved one who has settled himself in Me,
For no power can ever weaken My love that sets you free

Step up, step in and rest in the center of My love
For there waits perfect peace that will lift you high above
Coni

FATHER,

when I think of the great power used by You to part the Red Sea and to raise Lazarus from the dead, fear seems to become as a leaf in the wind. It is only when I turn my attention from Your exploits of old that I find my breath being sucked from my body when trouble knocks at my door. Let me not answer its knock until I have first rehearsed in my heart Your mighty acts. Only then can faith answer the door with me.

Psalm 107:29,30 "He calms the storm, so that it's waves are still. Then they are glad because they are quiet; so He guides them to their desired haven."

ANOINTED ARCHER

His aim is sharp
His arm strong
He hears your cry
Sending victory along

His bow is taut
Precision assured
His shafts of fire
Are His spoken Words

His Words of power
Are arrows of steel
Their sting of death
The enemy feels

Each target is met
Left weary and weak
Cursing and wailing
A hiding place to seek

With Sword in mouth
And arrows in hand
Our God reigns
Throughout every land

Our Archer is faithful
Never to sleep
He stands ever ready
Guarding His sheep
Coni

FATHER,

knowing that You are ever ready to come to my defense causes my heart to be at peace. It is not possible for You to fail, therefore, You will always hit the enemy dead center no matter how skilled he is in his strategies.

2 Samuel 22:15 "He sent out His arrows and scattered them; lightening bolts and He vanquished them."

ANSWER SEEDS

Sometimes prayers are whispered
Sometimes all night we've cried
It matters not to the Father
For each one, His Son has died

Your prayers are never measured
On a scale made by man
For every one that's offered
Is a treasure in His hand

They are music to His ears
These cries of various needs
Upon hearing every one
He sends down "answer seeds"

Some seeds grow up quickly
Others seem to take so long
Yet His answers ALWAYS fit
And His timing is NEVER wrong

Coni

LORD,

thank You that my prayers never float aimlessly about, but come directly before Your face. No matter how often I seem to repeat myself, each prayer is scooped up by You and placed deep in Your heart. Thank You for Your sweet patience. I ask You to help me with my patience in waiting, for the answer will come in due time. You are faithful to always hear and answer.

Psalm 102:17 "He shall regard the prayer of the destitute, and shall not despise their prayer."

AWAITING YOUR CALL

When trouble comes
He knows the way
He'll hover close
Without delay

No need to fear
He does not hide
Just call His name
He's at your side

His ears are keen
His eye's on you
He reaches His hand
To pull you thru

Cry out in boldness
Not whimpering doubt
Faith moves God
He'll heed your shout

Grab hold of strength
Clasp on to love
He'll not relent
Till you rise above
Coni

FATHER,

how blessed I am to have You waiting for the sound of my voice. It's as though You are forever sitting on the edge of Your Throne so as not to miss the smallest whimper from my heart. To know You never tire of hearing me call for help makes me want to lift my voice in praise instead of pleading. Thank You, Lord.

Jeremiah 33:3 "Call to Me, and I will answer you, and show you great and mighty things, which you do not know."

BIRTH OF A NEW DAY

The air floats fresh and cool and my coffee is fragrantly warm
All is well within my soul for a new day is now being born

The birds, melodious in praise, sing to the Master of love
Their songs cradle the amber sun gently lifting it high above

Flowers reach to touch His light, grass quickly drinks His dew
His voice caresses me, whispering, "My mercy is renewed"

I smell His sweet essence, I hear the quietness of His peace
My Lord has surrounded me and my heart awakens with ease

I welcome this new morn' awaiting my Lord's careful plans
In trust I'll face this day for I'm carved in His loving hands

The sun's kiss of warmth will grow as it dances higher yet
His gift of new chances unfolds, every need faithfully met

The Glory of His presence gently bathes my heart as I say,
"Thank You for letting me witness the birth of this new day."
Coni

FATHER,

how wonderful are the works of Your hands. Each day You perform Your talents before those who rise early enough to slip in and watch. The blessings that await those who come into Your studio as the sun begins to reveal what the moon held captive. Your sweet peace gently nudges the night back to its resting place and there we see and hear and smell the stirring of life once again. Thank You for the honor of being in Your audience, Lord.

Psalm 104:24 "O LORD, how manifold are Your works! In wisdom You have made them all. The earth is full of Your possessions"

BLESSED BANKS

I settled down on the banks
Of a softly singing stream
And stretched to see its treasures
As light rained down its gleam

It was so clear and cool
Its invitation I could hear
It beckoned me, "Come closer,
I am nothing you should fear."

Its song so soothed my heart
That I lost all sense of space
I reached to touch its wetness
And its mist refreshed my face

I knew my Lord was there
For I saw Him all about
He did not remain silent
Of His love the rocks cried out

I closed my tear-filled eyes
To whisper a prayer of thanks
For letting me be a witness
To His Majesty on the banks
Coni

FATHER,

I pray that I never fail to see the treasures of the world around me. Help me to cease from the bustle of life, even if it is for but a moment, to recognize that little piece of You in all that is around me. So often You speak of who You are through the wonders of nature. A true craftsman always puts some of Himself inside His craft. Help me to not only stop and smell the roses, but to see Your face there, too.

Romans 1:20 "For since the creation of the world His invisible attributes are clearly seen, being understood by the things that are made, even His eternal power and Godhead, so they are without excuse,"

CHRISTMAS GIFT

Your gift to man, THE HOLY ONE
Was sent in love, Your Beloved Son

He came so small, precious and sweet
Yet grew strong, an enemy to defeat

He walked in power and gave His life
Brought great peace, conquering strife

Mercy caused Him to walk this earth
Love brought Him death for our new birth

He came a babe, yet left as LORD
For eternity's days, He'll be adored

Let hearts be full and voices lift
To God in praise for His Christmas Gift
Coni

FATHER,

oh the hustle and bustle of the world at this time of year must sadden Your heart. Why has the man in the red suit overshadowed the Lord in the manger. Forgive me, Lord. May I bow my knee and look up to heaven for Your "Gift", and not bow my knee to look under the tree for my gift.

Isaiah 9:6 "For unto us a Child is born, unto us a Son is given; and the government will be upon His shoulder. and His name will be called Wonderful. Counselor, Mighty God, Everlasting Father, Prince of Peace."

CIRCUMCISED HEART

He reached and drew His Sword
And poised it over my heart
He knew He must cut quickly
Before new life could start

My heart was doomed from birth
To wander about as lost
So Jesus offered Himself
Even though He knew the cost

He cut with precision and care
The flesh from my heart fell.
He wrapped my wound in love
And pulled my feet from hell

A covenant is now in force
That will never fade away
He set my heart in His
And freed me from the grave

O Blessed Holy Sword
Your work was swift and sure
I now have a heart that's new
Kept safe, and strong, and pure
Coni

FATHER,

I lay myself upon Your altar of love and trust You to do a work in my heart. It is my desire to have spoken of me as it was of David, a heart like Yours, Father. I desire that the love in my heart is an exact copy of Your love, pure, free, and unconditional. I ask that You give me a heart that is resistant to hurt and selfishness, one that has great outflow ability, one that is not self-centered but giving-centered. I do not fear Your loving knife, Lord, for it brings me the desire of my heart – YOUR HEART.

Deuteronomy 30:6 "And the LORD your God will circumcise your heart and the heart of your descendants, to love the LORD your God with all your heart and with all your soul, that you may live."

CREATED TO FLY

His hand shaped my heart
His loved wrapped it tight
He set His fire upon me
And brought me thru the night

He breathed His life within
He cradled me in His grace
He took me from my fears
To a high and lifted place

He spoke to me of exploits
He covered me in His cocoon
He worked without tiring
To free me from painful gloom

I started out frail and small
But He changed me with His hand
He took me from a caterpillar
To a butterfly, dancing over land

Oh, thank You, Holy Father
For causing me to grow
For when I am as You dreamed
Then fulfillment I'll truly know
Coni

LORD,

may I never be so comfortable where I am, that I cease to push higher still. It is in my complacency that I remain unfinished. I am only whole when I continue to press toward Your calling and move out from where I am to where You are. Help me to see Your dream for me, for only then will I go from glory to glory.

The best is yet to come.

Philippians 3:14 "I press toward the goal for the prize of the upward call of God in Christ Jesus."

CREATION SPEAKS OF LOVE

God whispered to me today in a gentle blowing breeze
And showed how much He cares thru the beauty of the seas

He called me out by name in the bird's sweet songs of love
And gently kissed my face with a snowflake from above

He blessed my eyes with color in His vast array of flowers
And refreshed my weary brow with a gentle summer shower

He places within His work small pieces of His love
He rains down soothing light in the moon and stars above

He has no need for rainbows nor the leafy tall oak tree
He made them as His love gift and gave them to you and me

May we be ever mindful as we look upon His lands
Of His presence and His power thru the creation of His hands
Coni

FATHER,

when I look about at all that Your hands have made, from the peaks of the tallest mountain to the last little black dot on the ladybug, I am made aware of great detail.

If You care about such detail in these things created by Your spoken word, how much more You care about us who were hand made and God breathed. I am truly humbled by Your gifts around me.

Psalm 104:24 "O LORD, how manifold are Your works! In wisdom You have made them all. The earth is full of Your possessions-"

CRYING HEARTS HEARD

Their eyes so dark with fear, bodies bent and broken
They reached to us for alms, but God's Word is what was spoken

We saw such lack of purpose, their lives appeared a waste
Yet we knew we held the key, so God's love we gave with haste

Their houses small and tattered, some held together with rope
We talked of God's provision and gave to them His hope

God's heart is in this land, His love cradles this place
We brought with us His light and He covered them with grace

The bonds of death were broken for God's power was unleashed
Freedom found its mark as the Word of God was preached

The sea of hands then raised high unto the sky
reaching to grasp their miracle as their healing Lord passed by

We battled in the heavenlies, causing the enemy great strife
Deliverance now reigns free for we left with them His life
Coni

FATHER,

help me to remember that the fields are white with harvest and that salvation is not my private gift. You do not love me more than those around me. If it had not been for the sharing of someone else, I too would still be lost and dying. Cause a burning passion in my heart to share the Truth, just as this same passion burned in someone else's heart for me.
Love never keeps to itself.

*Matthew 25:40 "And the King will
answer and say to them,
'Assuredly, I say to you, inasmuch
as you did it to the least of these My
brethren, you did it unto Me."*

DO YOU HEAR HIM COMING?

Do you hear Him coming?
Can you smell His essence?
He brings with Him His grace
And peace escorts His presence

Fear not, My weary one
For I your Lord draw near
I reach to hold you close
To whisper of love in your ear

Look not unto thy past
For it's covered in My blood
Carry not the yoke of guilt
For mercy rides upon the flood.

Gaze deep into My eyes
And take from there My love
Reach out and touch My hand
And I'll lift thee high above.

Step into that holy place
That I have kept for thee
There rest and have thy being
From now through eternity.

Do you hear Him coming?
He's coming here for thee.
Coni

FATHER,

as it was with Adam in the garden in the cool of the day, even now You come daily to walk with me. I pray that I never hide from Your presence because of sin. Help me to remember the forgiveness that flows so freely from Your throne. I desire to hear Your voice and run to meet You without hesitation. Keep my ears sensitive to the whisper of Your loving voice. Thank You, Father that You desire to come for me every day.

Genesis 3:8,9 "And they heard the sound of the Lord God walking in the garden in the cool of the day....then the LORD God called to Adam and said to him, 'Where are you?'"

EASTER MORN

The sun awoke and rose
To take the night away
It shone softly on my face
Bringing light unto my day

The sun awoke and rose
And caused the earth to yawn
It kissed the flowers fair
And stroked the newborn fawn

The sun awoke and rose
And graced the meadows green
It climbed unto the heavens
And made the mountains gleam

Yet greater than all of this
Is the real truth of this day
And the new life that it brings
To those who kneel and pray

For this day in ages past
The "darkness" came to a close
"Light" was freed to every heart
For Gods' SON, Jesus, awoke and rose
Coni

LORD,

the first Easter morn so long ago is made fresh and new every year. New life was given to all mankind and for that I am so thankful. The quietness of this morning is in such contrast to the power that shook the earth when the stone rolled away. Only in You can there be peace and power at once. Thank You for dying, but more than that, thank You for rising.

Matthew 28:7 "And go quickly and tell His disciples that He is risen from the dead..."

FAITH'S VOICE

Sight may sometimes tell you
"Give up for all is lost."
But faith would say instead
"Hold on at any cost."

Sometimes our life long dreams
Crumble in a tattered pile
Heaped at our weary feet
Stealing our hopeful smile

Hold tight to His Word, wavering not
And His voice you will surely hear
It will shatter the screams of the dark
If you listen with faith, not fear

He calls things that are not
Into things that we see
By the decree of His holy mouth
He sets every doubt free

When you feel empty-handed
Give your "nothings" to the Lord
And watch Him transform them
Into touchable rewards
Coni

LORD,

what a powerful gift You gave me when You placed Your faith in me. Nothing pleases You more than when I am moved by it and not by what I see or feel or hear. Faith does not sit silently by and watch the enemy kill, steal and destroy. It shouts the shout of victory and when it is heard it becomes stronger yet. Help me to speak only that which causes You to move on my behalf.

Matthew 17:20 "Because of your unbelief; for assuredly, I say to you, if you have faith as a mustard seed you will say to this mountain, 'move from here to there,' and it will move; and nothing will be impossible for you."

FATHER'S DELIGHT

All that ye can see
The earth and stars above
I created just for thee
Because of My holy love

For I needed not the air
Nor the bird's sweet love songs
I needed not the flower fair
For thee alone, My heart longs

I laid for thee a carpet
A place for thee to rest
In all thy eyes have met
You'll find I gave My best

My love painted the land
My voice chiseled out the sky
My strength holds fast thy hand
My heart cradles your every cry

All creation is thy gift
All that ye touch and see
It is thy voice that lifts My heart
I have all I need in thee.
Coni

FATHER,

to know that You set all this in place for man is amazing to me. All that is, was made for me. As an expecting parent lovingly prepares for the arrival of their new child with great anticipation, so too, You, Father, prepared this place for Your children. No short cuts, no expenses spared, only perfection! May I never take for granted the love You poured into the place of my earthly dwelling. Seeing how wonderful this abode is makes me crave to be in my heavenly dwelling place with You.

Genesis 2:8 "The LORD God planted a garden eastward in Eden, and there He put the man whom He had formed."

FIRST THINGS FIRST

As the night slips back to it's hiding place
And the light steps in to bestow its grace
I hear the distant morning chorus
Of feathered friends You created for us

They chirp and sing and fluff their wings
As the light of dawn reveals the spring
They rush not off into their days,
Until they pause to give You praise

They beckon us to join their songs
Before we rush into humanities throngs
They know the value of praise and glory
And woo Your people to rejoice, not worry

Before the dawn their melodies start
For they know the love of the Creator's heart
Once their praises are lifted high
Off they wing to dance in the sky

May we, Your children, do no less
Than to begin each day by offering our best
To stop and pay the homage due
That rightfully, Lord, belongs to You
Coni

FATHER,

Your creation instinctively knows first things first. They do it without thought, without prodding, without expecting anything in return. They do it because it is part of their being. Oh Father, forgive me for rushing into my day without giving to You, who gave me this day, the glory due. Help me not to overlook the One who continually looks over me.

Psalm 34:1 "I will bless the Lord at all times; His praise shall continually be in my mouth."

GIFTS TO GIVE

Lord, when I stop and think
That there can be no more
You open up my heart
And freely begin to pour

At times I feel so full
And about to overflow
Then I see it is time
To share the love I know

You do not fill me up
To keep it tucked inside
But to touch another's heart
So in You they can abide

Your gifts to me are holy
Yet not for me alone
They are for helping others
To find their way back home

Lord, may I never harbor
What You've placed in me
But always pass it on
Setting the captives free
Coni

LORD,

help me to remember that the gifts

You have given to me are not for me

alone but for the world. Reveal to me

when, where, and how to use them

in order to bring You the greatest

glory, and meet the simplest of

needs. May I never forget that it's

when I give out of myself that I am

most fulfilled.

Ephesians 4:16 "from whom the whole body joined and knit together by what every joint supplies, according to the effective working by which every part does its share, causes growth of the body for the edifying of itself in love."

Go YE

Go ye child, into the dark
For many are crying there
Their hearts are torn and weary
For life has been unfair

Go ye child, tell them of LOVE
For their ears have not heard
They lay broken and battle worn
Needing My healing WORD

Go ye child, lift their burden
For all their hope is crushed
Their eyes are blind with lies
For the enemy has stolen much

Go ye child, bring My light
For they are bound in bleakness
Their feet are bruised and bleeding
They struggle in endless weakness

Go ye child, for you're My hands
Their tears you can surely dry
For life will flood their tired souls
When they know for them I died

Go ye child, and know in your heart
You will never be the same
For you will see the life you've given
When you share with them My Name
Coni

LORD,

Your heart holds dear those who are lost and dying. I ask that I share the same heart. It has been said that one carries a "burden" for the lost but Father give me eyes to see that I must carry a "love" for the lost. When I can see my heart carrying love and not a burden, then my call becomes one of joy, not dread. It becomes filled with opportunities, not obligations. Let it be that my soul is not satisfied until I,

"GO YE"

Mark 16:15 "Go into all the world and preach the gospel to every creature."

GOOD MORNING, LORD

Good morning, Lord of all
I lift my voice in love
I ask Your heart to be in me
and guide me from above

I place my heart in You
and offer my hands today
I'll go wherever You lead
and speak whatever You say

O' precious Holy Spirit
teach my heart of Him
Give me Godly wisdom
that keeps my soul from sin.

This is the day You've made
I will rejoice and praise
Help me give Your love to all
and keep me in Your ways

Send me those who hurt
show me what they feel.
Then let Your power rise
that comforts, lifts, and heals

I offer You all that I am
I place myself in Your hands
And when my day is done
I pray I fulfilled Your plans
Coni

FATHER,

may I never begin my day without my morning gift of love and adoration. You deserve my first words each day and my last words each night. You have blessed me with breath this day, so I give it back to You in praise. Walk with me and talk with me today. Help me to be Your hands, Your mouth, Your heart to this hurting world.

Romans 12:1 "I beseech you therefore, brethren by the mercies of God, that you present your bodies a living sacrifice, holy, acceptable to God, which is your reasonable service."

HARD PLACES

I saw a flower growing
In a most unusual place
Its face reached toward heaven
Beckoning for God's grace

I bent to examine it close
It seemed so all alone
Yet I knew God had touched it
For it grew from a crack in a stone

To my life my thoughts were drawn
And in my heart I know
That even in the "hard places"
God's love will make me grow
Coni

FATHER,

Your life dwells in me, therefore, wherever I find myself, I can trust in Your power to cause me to keep growing. I need not fear the hard dry places because You turn deserts into streams. You continually water me with Your presence.

Isaiah 58:11 "The Lord will guide you continually, and satisfy your soul in drought, and strengthen your bones; and you shall be like a watered garden, and like a spring of water, whose waters do not fail."

HE IS, "I AM"

He's faithful to the faithless
Abundance to the poor
Peace to the peaceful
The Answer at the door

He's love to the loving
Kindness to the kind
Hearing to the deaf
And sight to the blind

He's courage to the bold
Strength to the weak
Wisdom to the wise
The voice for those who speak

He's Savior to the saved
Forgiver of all sins
He's whatever is needed
Whenever you call to Him
Coni

FATHER,

when You spoke, "I Am who I Am",

all that was needed to be said was said.

To look elsewhere for what I need

is but a waste of time. You fill all in all.

You fit perfectly every time. You are the

Supplier of all supplies, anything else

leaves me lacking.

*Exodus 3:14 "And God said to Moses,
"I AM WHO I AM."*

HIS HEALING HEM

To touch the hem of His garment
frees spirit, body, and soul
for it's woven with His love
causing virtuous healing to flow

His hem is plain and simple,
its power hidden to the eye
yet when it's touched in faith
infirmities, yield and die

The holiness of His hem
carries anointing for mankind
it brings hope to the hopeless
and restores sight to the blind

His glory is never fading
His mercy renewed each day
His hem of wondrous grace
will never be pulled away

So, bow your knee before Him
His heart will heed your cry
reach out for His hem of love
as the Lord of all walks by.
Coni

LORD,

Your heart is consumed
with compassion for all
mankind. You remind me in
Your Word that You came to
destroy the works of the devil.
You have done this through
Your shed blood. This brought
healing to all who will reach
out to touch You. I thank You
that You are never out of my reach.

Matthew 14:36 "... and begged Him that they might only touch the hem of His garment. And as many as touched it were made perfectly well."

HIS MAJESTY'S THRONE

The heavens are full of His glory
He's the Rock on which to stand
He'll hold you sure and steady
When life is as shifting sand

His arms are not too short
Nor His answers ever wrong
He lifts you to the Father
Your name is in His song

He searches the earth to find
Hearts that are tried and true
He reaches to touch your face
Imparting His strength to you

With faith and expectant hope
Look up to His Majesty's throne
Rest on the promise He's given
To keep you till He takes you home
Coni

FATHER,

no matter where I am or what has come my way, if I look unto Your throne I will always find You on the edge of Your seat awaiting my call for help. From Your throne flows mercy, hope, forgiveness, help, strength and victory. I thank You that because of the shed blood of Jesus, I am able to approach this holy throne in confidence, for I know by your Word that grace waits for me there.

Psalm 145:5 "I will meditate on the glorious splendor of Your majesty, and on Your wondrous works."

HOLY SEED

Come eat My child, I have all you need
For wisdom is found in My "Holy Seed"

There is not a care that I cannot ease
When you partake of My "Holy Seed"

I send love your way that sustains and frees
That's carefully nestled in My "Holy Seed"

My presence awaits when on bended knee
And peace is uncovered in My "Holy Seed"

Strength for the day you need not plead
For I will supply it through My "Holy Seed"

Victory comes running when My WORD you heed
For there's grace and guidance in My "Holy Seed"

Forgiveness and mercy are loudly decreed
For love is the heartbeat of My "Holy Seed"

Partake of My WORD and you will see
Fulfillment of heart in My "Holy Seed"
Coni

FATHER,

the anointing of Your Word

overpowers any situation I can

face. It is a seed that requires

planting into a fertile, receptive

heart. Your Word is a seed of

holiness and truth. It will produce

a bumper crop of quality Godly fruit

because You Yourself perform it

on my behalf. May I never miss

a planting season, Lord.

*Luke 8:11 "Now the parable is this:
The seed is the WORD OF GOD."*

IS YOUR MIDDLE NAME JONAH?

In our hearts imbedded deep, God's call was given to each.
To some He said, Be My hands, to others He said, Go preach

He asks of us to hear and obey and step out into His ways
For when we do, peace finds a home and dwells with us each day

To hear His call and walk away brings storms and mighty winds
These come to us on Mercy's wings to lead us from our sins

His love flows hard and strong though rebellion is our guide
He shines His light in every place proving there's nowhere to hide

It's only when we run no more and surrender to His call
That our heart finds its rest and our feet no longer fall

His hand is not too short nor His ear too heavy to hear
To save those who turn and repent, again He draws them near

Hide no longer from His voice but stand ready to obey
For then your God can rescue you from rebellion's grip and decay

His love will seek you out for His plans can never fail
Even if it means for you, three days inside a whale
Coni

FATHER,

how many times have I heard

Your heart ask me to do Your bidding

yet I turned and ran the other way.

What futility, for when I get as far

from Your will as I can, I find that

You are there waiting for me.

Lord, I pray that Your love will place a

Whale in my path as You did for Jonah.

May my food be as it was for Jesus,

"to do Fathers will"

no matter how it tastes to my flesh.

Psalm 95:7,8 "...Today, if you will hear His voice: do not harden your hearts as in the rebellion, as in the day of trial in the wilderness."

JESUS PRAYS FOR ME

A truth I found today
A truth that set me free
I found it in God's Word
That Jesus prays for me

It wasn't enough to my Lord
To suffer, bleed, and die
For me today He lifts His voice
And the Father hears His cry

Not a moment passes by
That He fails to lift me high
He calls my name in the heavens
Drawing me ever nigh

He prayed for me while on earth
He prays for me yet still
He says He will never cease
For it's the Father's will

Yes, a truth I found today
A truth that set me free
I found it in God's Word
That Jesus prays for me
Coni

LORD JESUS,

Your love for me is never ceasing. When I stop to think of all that You did at Calvary, this would have been enough for me, yet it was not for You. You still do not rest. Your constant intercession for me to this very day, is overwhelming to my heart. May I be found as faithful to You as You are to me.

Hebrews 7:25 "Therefore He is also able to save to the uttermost those who come to God through Him, since He ever lives to make intercession for them."

JOURNEY TO HEALING

This journey, LORD, brings unrest and fear stirs my soul,
But because Your love carries me, I know with You I must go

Anxious thoughts cause me to waver on this path to the unknown,
But the painful wounds will only grow, if kept hidden and left alone

My heart wants to see, my mind understand, before leaving with Thee
But faith in Your touch nudges me on, in assurance that I'll be set free

What will be found around twisted bends, what's hidden in my soul,
I know by Your Word, I must loose all of self, before I'm finally whole

The dross that rises from Your refining fire causes my heart to grieve,
Yet without this fire set ablaze by Your love, I will not be relieved

Your light must shine on all the dark places before my journey is done,
But I know inside if there is no revealing, my healing can never come

So trusting You, I heed the call and step onto Your altar of love,
I avail myself to Your holy will, knowing mercy flows from above

Take my hand, Lord, and lead me to where grace and victory are stored,
I trust in Your love and lean fully on You, for You are my healing Lord
Coni

FATHER,

I know that before I can go deeper into You, I must present myself to You for pruning. My heart yearns to be rid of all the unfruitfulness in my life. I know that Your refining work requires a willing heart. I do not fear the cutting away for it is always done in loving perfection.

Psalm 51:12 "Restore to me the joy of Your salvation, and uphold me with Your generous Spirit."

JUST WANTED YOU TO KNOW

I chose you ages ago
To redeem your life from the pit
I yearn to show you My face
In My presence I call you to sit

It makes no difference, My child
If you have walked away
My love's buried in your heart
And there it will always stay

You made choices to please self
You've followed a dark road
Yet I've never turned My back
Except to carry your load

Though sin has wracked your life
My hand has not let go
Your face is ever before Me, child
I just wanted you to know
Coni

FATHER,

Your grace, Your mercy, Your unconditional love floods my soul. To know that Your greatest desire is for me to experience these gifts is too high, I cannot attain it. My heart rejoices so in the truth that You, the creator of all that is, craves to reveal the depths of Your perfect heart to this flawed heart. Knowing this brings me great comfort.

Psalm 103:1-3 "Bless the Lord, O my soul; and all that is within me, bless His Holy Name! Bless the LORD, o my soul, and forget not all His benefits: who forgives all your iniquities, who heals all your diseases,"

LORD OF BLESSING

He blesses those who love
and walk in His ways
He blesses those who trust
in His faithfulness each day

He blesses those of faith
who stand firm and strong
He blesses those who praise
even when nights are long

He blesses those who lean
on Him who saves the lost
He blesses those who give
no matter what the cost

He blesses those who cry
and turn to Him in trial
He blesses those who believe
whose heart holds no denial

He is the Lord of blessing
He is the Lord of love
He is the Lord of peace
He IS our Lord above
Coni

FATHER,

Your arms overflow with goodness for me. Your blessings pour unhindered from Your open hands into my life. Blessings that continuously fall from your overstocked storehouse above seem to know when to begin their descent so as to arrive into my life in due season. Perfect timing for a **PERFECT FIT.**

Deuteronomy 28:2 "And these blessings shall come upon you and overtake you, because you obey the voice of the LORD your God:"

LOVING LIBERATOR

When in me there is no strength to take the steps I need
He lifts me to His shoulders and from fear my heart is freed

When I face mountains tall that block my faith-filled view
He covers me with HIS grace and my courage is renewed

When my fingers loosen their grip from holding fast to His hands
He takes me in His loving arms and carries me to promised lands

When my ears are deafened by lies and confusion freezes my soul
His power surrounds me completely and again His voice I know

When in battle my life is threatened and peace is lost in the dark
He takes His stand before me and the arrows miss their mark

When my cries cannot be stilled and my heart lays torn and bare
He gathers each broken piece and repairs it with Fatherly care

So when each day has been spent and my pillow cradles my head
I raise my voice in grateful praise for in Him I'm kept and led
Coni

FATHER,

each day I need Your presence.
Each day I need Your love. This
is the only way that I will remain
standing when day is done. You are
ever ready with Your freeing touch
to take me through each day. Your
grace ushers me into victory in
every situation.

Psalm 18:19 "He also brought me out into a broad place; He delivered me because He delighted in me."

MERCY'S MISSION

There is a place in heaven where Mercy doth reside
A place of royal honor kept ready for "The Bride"

This gift of endless Mercy stands eager to supply
God's peace and restoration at the sound of every cry

God's Mercy is ever watchful from her heavenly home above
for a place to lay her head and settle in with love

This Mercy carries with her, healing, hope, and life
Her power is relentless at dispelling fear and strife

God's Mercy is no weakling but graceful, bold, and strong
The enemy flees in terror at the sound of her victory song

So call upon God's Mercy and you will see her ride
Swiftly and determined to stand ready at your side

Mercy gives herself freely ever ready to do her part
For this place where she dwells is in the center of God's heart
Coni

FATHER,

where would the world be without Your limitless mercy? Mercy caused You to look past my failures and reach deep into Your heart and pull out Your Son Jesus. You set within Him, forgiveness and love beyond measure. Your mercy is still as fresh today as then. Each day it stands fresh and new waiting to be poured out. Your mercy is not satisfied until it comes to the aid of Your people. I thank you that I don't need to beg for it, I just need to accept it. It is like a faithful companion that never grows weary of being with me. It is impossible for it to run out for it is new each morning, watching for any opportunity to cover me. Thank You, Father

Lamentations 3:22,23 "Through the LORD'S mercies we are not consumed, because His compassions fail not. They are new every morning..."

"MEETING PLACE"

I call out your name, I desire your face
Will you not come, child, to our "Meeting Place"

There's much to be said tender moments to share
Great wisdom awaits for our gathering there

Secrets are unveiled, guidance to lead
Worry is conquered as Truth is decreed

Holiness is transferred, power is endued
Loneliness is vanquished when I am pursued

My presence is stirring, reaching to hold
Restoration's accomplished as My glory unfolds

There My heart speaks of the love that it carries
Your praise is My passion therefore, daily I tarry

So answer My call, child, obtain mercy and grace
and heart peace you'll find at our "Meeting Place"
Coni

FATHER,

how can it be that You

desire my presence daily?

The failings of my life are

ever before You, yet you call

unto me to come. May I

never take for granted Your

mercy and passion for me.

May I never be so selfish

that I keep You waiting or

fail to show up at all.

1 Corinthians 1:9 "God is faithful, by whom you were called into the fellowship of His Son, Jesus Christ our Lord."

MY ALL IN ALL

My eyes will lead thee
My voice will soothe
My hand will guide thee
When I am pursued

My joy will lift thee
My comfort will ease
My power will renew thee
And bring lasting peace

My heart will hold thee
My goodness will provide
My faithfulness guards thee
In My wings ye can hide

My WORD lights the way
My arms draw thee close
My love overflows thee
For thee I have chose

My hope pulls thee out
My strength will set free
Let rest keep thy heart
For I'll not forsake thee
Coni

LORD,

**to look anywhere other than
to You for my every need is
fruitless. You are the sustainer
of all there is. You keep the earth
from falling through the sky.
All that is, is because You caused it.
How can I even entertain the thought
of finding the answers anywhere
outside of You? To look elsewhere
is to fall into idolatry. May I never
bring a tear to Your eye because I
turned my eyes from you.**

*Philippians 4:19 "And my God shall supply
all your need according to His riches
in glory by Christ Jesus."*

NIGHT BATTLES

It's in the midst of the night
That battles rage so strong
And fear encamps all about
Deafening ears to the Hero's song

Darkness escorts the deadly foes
Of confusion, loss, and pain
It causes hearts to seize in fear
And voices to be lost in the rain

Just look unto His Holy Hill
Though eyes are tired and weak
From there the answer will come
And lay at your weary feet

Heaven will open its gates
And upon the clouds He will come
Heeding each muttered cry
Wielding sword till the battle is done

It's in battle that God comes near
Presenting Himself as Champion
Standing victorious before His foe
Leaving peace to be your companion
Coni

LORD,

the enemy always seems to hit

the hardest when night falls.

Rest does not come easy because

the quiet of the night seems to

magnify the noise of the turmoil.

Help me, Lord, to hold on to You

not only through the darkness

of the night but also through

the darkness of soul.

Psalm 55:18 "He has redeemed my soul in peace from the battle which was against me..."

POTTER'S CLAY

I am the Potter's clay
Placed on His loving wheel
I'll trust His gentle hands
Not what I see, or feel

He has me there on purpose
To mold and shape my life
He caresses out the stones
That would later cause me strife

His hands are never rough
His eyes ever focused on me
He turns me at His will
Setting all of my fears free

He'll not cease from His work
Nor from His wheel turn
Until He sees in me
That for which He yearns

The fire of His furnace
Burns to make me pure
And only when I'm complete
Will I be able to endure

He gently lifts me up
Placing His finishing touch
Stamping upon my soul
"I love you very much"
Coni

FATHER,

may I never be released

from Your wheel until I am

as You desire. Help me to

never choose to step down

before Your refining fire

seals me. For only then will

I be able to hold the anointing

that Your vessels are designed

to carry.

*Isaiah 64:8 "But now, O Lord, You are our Father;
we are the clay, and You our potter; and all
we are the work of Your hand."*

PRECIOUS PEACE

There's no place to run
Too tired to stand
I reach for my God
He takes hold of my hand

My tears stain my cheeks
And fall to my breast
I step into love
And He gives me His rest

My heartbeat is weak
My breath all but gone
I then hear His voice
As He sings me love songs

No trial too great
No valley too deep
That His love cannot reach
And bring me sweet peace

So peace be still
For the Lord is near
His comfort flows freely
Consuming all fear
Coni

FATHER,

sometimes the wind blows me off balance,

tearing at my faith, but You rise to my

rescue and anchor me into Your heart.

The winds must come for they are part of

life's testing, so I ask not for them to

stop but only for You to always remain

within reach.

*Isaiah 26:3 "You will keep him in perfect peace,
whose mind is stayed on You..."*

SLEEPLESS KEEPER

When trials come to visit, peace stands to do her part
For the Lord of all that is, is the keeper of my heart

When fear comes with its grip strength pours from above
For the Lord of all that is, is the keeper of my love

When sickness tries to steal, healing conquers the strife
For the Lord of all that is, is the keeper of my life

When sin knocks at my door, deliverance comes my way
For the Lord of all that is, is the keeper of my day

In perfect peace I rest, in love I am kept whole
For the Lord of all that is, is the keeper of my soul

My Keeper never sleeps, He's vigilant and strong
He hovers over my spirit singing His victory song
Coni

FATHER,

how it comforts me knowing that I am kept by the One who is pure holiness. People keep only those things that are valuable to them personally. When I think that I am valuable enough for You, the King of kings and the Lord of lords, I am filled with thanksgiving. To know I am treasured by You is overwhelming.

Psalm 121:4,5 "Behold, He who keeps Israel shall neither slumber nor sleep. The LORD is your keeper; the LORD is your shade at your right hand.

SOMETIMES TEARS CAN SMILE

*Sometimes it seems so hard when their hand slips away
and we no longer see the smile that graced our eyes each day*

*Sometimes life takes us places that we desire not to trod
but if we hold fast to faith it will show us the face of God*

*Sometimes grief comes knocking refusing to depart
but if we lean on Jesus joy will find our heart*

*Sometimes understanding is fleeting as to the "why" of our loss
but when we draw near to the Savior, peace is found at the Cross*

*Sometimes our tears flow strong seeking a place to land
but they never go unnoticed for God holds each one in His hand*

*Sometimes we must say goodbye to the one we cherished so
but God then sends His Spirit so sweet comfort we can know*

*Sometimes loneliness holds us but God's strength will set us free
for then we hear Him whisper, "Your loved-one rests with Me."
Coni*

FATHER,

through the pain, through the tears, through the confusion and the fear, if I but look past all the feelings that are whirling around me, I will see that a precious thing has happened to the ones I love. They have not ceased to live, they have only begun to live. May I never be so selfish as to want to pull them from Your loving arms.

Psalm 116:15 "Precious in the sight of the LORD is the death of His saints."

SPRING'S ESCORTS

With winter's surrender and snow tucked away
We hear spring's arrival thru birds singing praise

They usher in warmth with the newness of life
As they flurry about free of worry and strife

They know their Creator will see to their need
Thru His evidence of love that He scatters as seeds

They know their purpose and the Master's great plans
And trust in the gentleness of His heart and His hands

They give all they are as an offering of praise
To the faithful One watching over their nights and their days

Can we do no less for our Father above
When in newness of life we walk into His love
Coni

FATHER,

all of Your creation brings the praise due Your name, yet man, who is dearest to Your heart often keeps silent. Oh may Your forgiveness never cease. I, who have been bought and redeemed, seem to take for granted what You have done for me. I go about my day in self-centeredness often forgetting to stop and give You my first thoughts. May I never forget to lift my voice first thing in the morning, to give You thanks and praise for considering me more valuable than the birds of the air.

*Matthew 6:26 "Look at the birds of the air,
for they neither sow nor reap nor gather
into barns; yet your heavenly Father
feeds them. Are you not of more value
than they?"*

STILLER OF THE STORM

Keep watch upon the Lord for the earth He did form
His power toward you is great, He's the "Stiller" of the storm

No matter the trial to face, no matter the path to trod
Hold fast to the Master's hand, trust in the love of your God

Tears will come and go, fear will try to steal
But keep your eyes on the Father, then His peace you'll feel

His arm is not too short, His love flows free and strong
He rises to heed your cry and deliverance is sent along

He never tires of your voice, He never turns away
He bathes you with His presence when praise is sent His way

So keep watch upon your Lord for the earth He did form
His power toward you is great, He's the "Stiller" of your storm
Coni

Father,

You never promised there

would not be storms in my

life, but You did promise to

be the One who quiets my heart

in the midst of them. It is You

who causes me to have the strength

to remain standing when the clouds

fade away. Your Presence is the

anchor of my heart.

Exodus 33:14 And He said, "My Presence will go with you, and I will give you rest."

TRUST IN TURMOIL

When voices seem loud and my mind needs rest
I'll cleave to my Lord for He gives me His best

When wisdom is needed for answers unknown
I'll climb on His lap where light is shown

When my soul is weary and battle fatigued
I'll reach for His Word and strength is freed

When it seems no way out and my heart lays bare
I'll enter His presence and secrets He'll share

When worry consumes me and I yearn for peace
His arms pull me close and my heart is at ease

When I tug at His heart needing mercy to rise
He answers me quickly and stills all my cries

He's my Lord and my God, my Comfort, my Grace
I'll trust in His love till we meet face to face
Coni

FATHER,

when the world around me pulls at every side and it looks as though everything around me is out of control, **THERE YOU ARE.** You are mightier than the noise of many waters. You are the source for whatever I need, so let the winds blow and the storms rage, for I will always find my peace in the One who is always in control.

Psalm 29:11 "The LORD will give strength to His people; The LORD will bless His people with peace."

UNWAVERING WISDOM

Wisdom to know what step to take
And the courage to see it thru
Comes from the God of love
Who gives liberally unto you

The way may seem dimly lit
Your feet too heavy to lift
Yet God gave the measure of faith
His tiny mustard seed gift

His Word stands ready and alert
Impossible at failing
Waiting to hear your lifted voice
In praise and not in wailing

His Wisdom is eager to comply
And penetrate your heart
If you will ask unwaveringly
She'll come and not depart

Fear not the road beyond the bend
For Wisdom has paved a way
She speaks to you from God's heart
Bringing you courage each day
Coni

FATHER,

Your Word says that wisdom is the principle thing. It was the only thing asked for by Solomon, yet because he asked for wisdom, You gave him much more besides. Your wisdom seeks out all hidden things, all things that lie in wait for a chance to bring me down. Wisdom craves to be had by all, may I not disappoint her.

Proverbs 4:5,6 "Get wisdom! Get understanding! Do not forget, nor turn away from the words of my mouth. do not forsake her, and she will preserve you."

VOICE OF SILENCE

The silence hedged me in, my heart peace did caress
I uttered not a word bowing before His stillness

I wondered what was next, I yearned to be consumed
In His holy presence my spirit was perfumed

No words were spoken out, no song sung to the sky
In quietness I was bathed as my loving Lord drew nigh

My ears heard not a word yet His voice entered inside
The Holy One of heaven settled in and did abide

Fear not the stillness heard, it beckons clear and plain
His voice does sweetly soothe as He gently sings your name

Be still and know He's God, though not a sound is made
His voice He'll hide within you and His love will never fade
Coni

FATHER,

why does the stillness seem to cause many to fear? Is it because of what we might hear from your heart? Oh, I pray Lord that I never draw back from that still small voice that speaks to every corner of my heart. You are a God of great power, yet when it comes time to beckon me close, your voice is but a wooing whisper. Help me to remember that there is strength in the stillness.

1 Kings 19:11,12 "...but the LORD was not in the wind; and after the wind an earthquake, but the LORD was not in the earthquake; and after the earthquake a fire, but the LORD was not in the fire; and after the fire a still small voice."

WARRIOR ON THE HILL

There in the distance it stood
a symbol of glory yet shame
Its roughness brought us tenderness
releasing the power of the Name

It stood as a warrior in battle
battered yet able to stand
It spoke of the victory it offered
to all throughout every land

Though many would not take hold
of its truth wrapped in glory
It shouts with a voice of triumph
the Father's Salvation Story

Yes, there in the distance it stood
the blood stained victorious Cross
It reaches to offer its love gift
of forgiveness to all who are lost

Coni

LORD JESUS,

the Father sent You to earth

to battle for my heart. You willingly

and knowingly said yes. You then

stepped out of glory to stand in shame

for me. You laid down deity and took

up sin. I failed and You agreed to take

the fall. Yes, You came to battle on my

behalf and Your weapon of choice was

THE CROSS.

*1 Corinthians 1:18 "For the message of the cross
is foolishness to those who are perishing,
but to us who are being saved it is the
power of God/"*

WATCHFUL WARRIOR

The mighty Warrior on His valiant steed
Is ever watchful for the sign
To descend and meet man's needs
When it's the Father's time.

He'll mount up and wing His way
To the earth imprisoned by sin.
And redeem His own on that day
In a battle only He can win.

Fear not, oh weak and trembling heart
For the Warrior knows your name
And from this earth He'll not depart
Till He's freed you from all pain.

He'll raise His mighty two-edged Sword
To defeat the enemy at your side
And lay before you a great reward
Then to the Father you both will ride.
      Coni

LORD,

how I look forward to

that day when You come to take

Your faithful home to dwell

eternally with You. Together

we will ride to that place where

wholeness lives, oh what blessed

assurance! How great is the peace

of my heart knowing that when the

Father's time is complete, You will

be my "Knight in Shining Armor"

and come to whisk me home.

Psalm 34:15 "The eyes of the LORD are on the righteous..."

WHISPER OF HIS SPIRIT

When your heart is weary and spent
And all your plans lay undone
The whisper of His Spirit
Gently woos unto you, "Come"

When trials press you hard
And cause your peace to run
The whisper of His Spirit
Gently woos unto you, "Come"

When your soul feels alone
And the darkness hides the sun
The whisper of His Spirit
Gently woos unto you, "Come"

If you would have ears to hear
You'll find faith has begun
For the whisper of His Spirit
Always woos unto you, "Come"
Coni

FATHER,

how so like You to send Your Holy Spirit to me with His endless wooing. I pray my ears keep sharp and my heart stays still so that I miss not one of His calls. You are faithful to woo, Lord, may I be faithful to press in, for when I do our hearts melt together making it impossible to tell where one begins and the other ends.

Psalm 27:8 "When You said, 'Seek My face,' My heart said to You. "Your face, LORD, I will seek."

THE WORD IS GOD

To seek God's Word is to seek His face
For they are the same by His Holy Grace

The beginning of time was spoken to life
By His Word of love He brought forth His Light

The Word is the Lord, it cannot be denied
It's His precious voice that's been tested and tried

When you need His touch, reach for The Bible
It is your source for complete survival

When your heart cries, "Lord, I need You near"
Grab hold of His Word and find peace not fear

Climb into His Word and you're in His arms
Abide in it daily, be kept from sin's charms

Yes, He is His Word and His Word is He
Take hold of this truth and you'll always be free
Coni

FATHER,

may I never look lightly

upon Your Word, for if I do

then I look lightly upon You.

How blessed I am to be able to

hold You in my hands, hear Your

voice and see You before me when

I open up Your Holy Bible. Time

in Your Word is time in

Your heart.

*John 1:14 "and the Word became flesh
and dwelt among us, and we beheld
His glory, the glory as of the only begotten
of the Father, full of grace and truth."*

NO MISTAKE

I saw the Lord on His throne and there was a great joy about Him. I could see that there was something very important going on. All of heaven, the angels and the saints of God who have gone on home before us, were going about the day's business. Everyone has a purpose in heaven as well as here on earth. There was hubbub all about, laughing, singing, praising, worship, projects being worked on, children playing, preaching and teaching of the ways of the Lord, eating and dancing. Did you know that all of the things we enjoy on earth are in heaven, only in their perfect state? God is a God of pleasure and He knows how to create what pleases Him. As these servants of God went about their day, they were so intent on their work and so filled with joy that they seemed unaware of the goings on around them. Each was fulfilling what God had entrusted them him. I then saw the Lord do something that intrigued me. I had to get a better look, so I immediately focused all my attention on Him. He stood up and reached inside His robe (at least that is what I thought) but when I looked closer, I saw that He had reached deep within Himself. As a matter of fact He had reached into the very center of His heart and pulled off a piece. It was beating with the same rhythm as His and His life-blood was flowing through it. He then took this living piece of His heart and cupped it in both hands and approached what looked like a huge slide. This slide started in the Throne room and came to an end on earth. When the Father got to the top of the slide He paused and called out to all of heaven. His voice thundered from one end to the other, not one ear was out of His reach.

    All of heaven came to a halt. All heads turned towards the Father and a hush fell. When everyone looked in the Father's direction, they saw Him motion for them to come and see. An excitement fell on the heavenly beings for they knew what all this meant. They all rushed over to the Father and stood at what looked like a banister overlooking the slide where they could easily see from top to bottom. When the Lord knew He had everyone's undivided attention, He took the piece of His beating heart and gently caressed it and shaped it and wrapped it up in His love. We all watched as the Father gazed at the treasure in His hand with such affection that many of us wept. Then He bent down and laid His love down on the slide and let it go. In an instant, the Father was at the end of the slide with arms outstretched and great joy and pride on His glorious face.

    He watched intently as His treasure descended, not taking His eyes off of it for a second. We could not see all the work that was going on as it made its way down but we knew that perfection was about to be displayed. Then the time had come.
The time that all of heaven had stopped to witness. The Father scooped up His manifested love, held it high for all to see and we all gasped at the wonderful sight. Once again all of heaven was silent, then, an explosion of praise and applause broke out. Words like, "beautiful, awesome, perfect" began to flood the heavenly realm. The Father slowly turned in a circle for all to see what He had done, not wanting anyone to miss His wonder.

It was as if heaven could not stop its applause and shouts of excitement until we saw the Father lower His treasure to cradle it close to His heart once again. As He was holding it close, I saw a small tag tenderly tied around its ankle but I could not see what was written there. Then the Father began moving towards a woman and laid His love gift in her arms. Heaven once again became silent.

As He moved away I could see the tag clearly and tears streamed down my face. Written there were three letters that were scrolled by the Father's own hand. These letters that were lovingly and boldly written with no regrets or shame on the Father's part, read Y-O-U. Oh, don't you see, YOU were part of the Father's heart. All of heaven waited in anticipation for YOU. All of heaven came to a halt to witness YOUR birth. The passion the Father has for YOU has never lessened from the time He pulled YOU out of His heart to this very day. "How can that be?" You say, "How can I be that cherished? Doesn't He know about me? Hasn't He seen what has become of me?" The answer is, yes, He does know and, yes, He has seen but all He cares about is that YOU are a part of Him and any part of Him is holy and worthy and eternally loved.

After seeing all that He so graciously allowed me to witness, He told me to tell everyone that this vision was true and it was about them. YOU are His heart, YOU, just as you are right now. YOU are the focus of His love and attention. YOU are His pride and joy. Yes, YOU.

Coni

MY CHILD

I know everything about you. (Ps.139:1) I have numbered the very hairs on your head.(Mt.10:30) I created you in My own image (Gen.1:27) and formed you in your mothers womb. (Jer.1:5) I have written all the days of your life down in My Book. (Ps.139:16) You are My very own offspring. (Acts17:28) My love for you is everlasting and I draw you to Myself with loving-kindness continually. .(Jer.31:3) Our lives are completely intermingled (1Jn.4:16) for I am in you and you are in Me (Jn.17:21) and I have placed My own love within you. (1Jn.3:1)

I give you only good and perfect gifts (Jam.1:17) and I will never change that. (Jer.32:40) My plans for you are always plans for good, (Jer.29:11) so do not worry about the things of life. (Mt.6:31-33) You are always foremost in My thoughts. (Ps.139:17,18) I rejoice over you with singing and will quiet you with My love. (Zeph.3:17)

You are My very own special treasure (Ex.19:5) that I chose before I even created the world. (Eph.1:4) I will give you the desires of your heart (Ps.37:4) because I placed them there. (Phil.2:13) I am more than able to do beyond anything you can dare to think or imagine. (Eph.3:20,21)

I am always there with you to comfort you in the hard times, (1Cor.1: 4) to be your place of safety and strength, (Ps.46:1) to mend your broken heart and seal up the hurts from others. (Ps.147:3) I gather you into My arms and carry you close to My heart. (Is.40:11) I wipe away every tear from your eyes and take away all the pain. (Rev.21:4) If you will let Me, I can turn all of your sadness into joy. (Ps.30:11)

I cause you to easily go down paths that would be hard if not impossible by yourself. (Ps.18:32,33) You are able to run against all odds and jump any obstacle, (Ps.18:29) because with Me you can do all things. (Phil.4:13)

If you stay close to Me, you will find great pleasures and be filled with joy. (Ps.16:11) Know that you are never out of My reach (Is.49:16) and never too far for Me to save you. (Is.59:1)

Be at peace when you sleep for even then I stand over you singing My songs of deliverance, (Ps.32:7) yes even then I hide you in the secret place of My presence. (Ps.31:20) I surround you as a shield (Ps.5:12) and when you wake you will see that I have kept you safe, (Ps.3:5) for I have set you apart for Myself (Ps.4:3) and nothing will ever separate us. (Ps.8:38,39)

Lean on Me and I will keep you in perfect peace when your mind rests on Me alone, (Is.26:3) when you are not moved by what you see. (Ps.46:2,3,5) Trust in the words I speak to you for they are tested and prove to be true (Ps.13:6) and will come to pass, not one of them will fail. (Josh.23:14)

Do not waver at My promises but be fully convinced that I can and want to do them, (Rm.4:20,21) for when I do My works who can reverse them? (Is. 43:13)

Know that My power works on your behalf, the same power that raised Christ from the dead, (Eph.1:19,20) so be strong in the power of My might (Eph.6:10) for it enables you to overcome, not be overcome. (1Jn.5:4,5) I am in you and I am greater than anything you will ever face. (1Jn.4:4) I supply all that you need and have all the answers to the things that come before you. (Phil. 4:19)

I am at your side every moment, (Ps.118:6) so don't be afraid of the things you hear, (Ps.112:7) just keep your eyes on Me (Heb.12:2) no matter what confusing things are going on around you because I am greater than what you hear. (Ps.93:4) I cause the storms in your life to be still (Mt.8:26) and I bring you through every time. (Is.43:2) You never have to worry about Me leaving you alone (Josh.1:5) not knowing which way to go or what to do. (Ps.32:8)

So come unto Me, child, for there and only there will you find rest (Mt.11:28) and that rest is yours for all time. (Heb.4:9)

I love you (1Jn.4:19),
Your Father (Mt. 23:9, Jn.1:12)

AUTHOR'S NOTE

I pray that your time here in,

"HIS HAMMOCK IN THE SHADE",

has been a time of comfort and peace.

It has been my deepest desire to help bring

you to a place where you can feel the

holiness of God's presence, to help you

to see that God is not untouchable.

He desires to visit with you intimately

daily. He yearns to share secrets

with His children, If you have not known

the Father in this personal way, I pray that

having read this collection of poems, letting

them touch that personal place in your heart,

you too, will be able to say,

"I HAVE TOUCHED THE FACE OF GOD.
Coni

GOD'S "LOVE PLAN"

There will be a day when we all will truly be face to face with the God of all holiness. When we do, we will hear Him say to us, "What have you done with My Son, Jesus?" Your answer to this question will be the difference as to whether you will spend eternity in heaven bathing in the Father's love, or in hell separated from everything that is good.

God has a "LOVE PLAN". This plan was put in place for you before You were even born. His plan made a way for you to live with Him for all time. You can not be good enough to earn this "LOVE PLAN" nor bad enough to have it taken away from you, the only role you have to play in it is to accept it as your very own.

God's "LOVE PLAN" is, JESUS. If you have not received Jesus as your personal Lord and Savior, I pray you will do so now. Asking Jesus into your heart will settle the answer that you will give the Father on that day when you meet with Him face to face.

Pray this prayer out loud and enter into God's heart.

Lord Jesus, I receive You as my Lord and Savior. I ask you to come and live in my heart. I believe You died on the cross for me and rose again. Fill me with Your Holy Spirit so that I may live my life for You. In Jesus' name, Amen

WELCOME TO THE FAMILY OF GOD!

SALVATION VERSES

Romans 10:9,10,13

"...if you confess with your mouth the Lord Jesus and believe in your heart that God has raised Him from the dead, you will be saved. For with the heart one believes unto righteousness, and with the mouth confession is made unto salvation. For "whoever calls on the name of the LORD shall be saved."

John 1:12

"...But as many as received Him, to them He gave the right to become children of God, to those who believe in His name..."

*I would love to hear what God has done for you.
You may email me at;*

heart_to_hand@hotmail.com

GOD BLESS YOU, CONI

www.ingramcontent.com/pod-product-compliance
Lightning Source LLC
LaVergne TN
LVHW041710060526
838201LV00043B/665